Introduction

The United States is probably the most diverse country in the world. Not only is its citizenry made up of peoples from many lands, but its terrain varies from the deserts of Arizona to the sea cliffs of Maine, from the swamps of Florida to the tundra of Alaska. The histories of the fifty states are also unique. Each state has its special qualities that distinguish it from the other forty-nine. This book will help you highlight those qualities for your students by engaging them in fun, hands-on, and challenging activities that require them to use many different talents and intelligences.

The activities in this book are organized around a central topic, studying your state, but they approach it from different perspectives. I believe it is important to provide a natural link between the different areas of the curriculum whenever possible. When links are established between the content areas, meaning is generated, and your students discover that the skills they are learning have applications beyond just getting answers right on a test. They will become intent on finding out the answers to the questions they are asking to satisfy their own curiosity, rather than just because they were told, "Because it's important to learn this."

So look through this book and try to find ways in which you can link subject areas. For instance if you are studying graphing in math, you might have students create the 3-D graph when studying your state's population (see page 20). If you are studying ecology in science, you can focus on ways to improve your state's environment as you complete the ecology circle book activity (see page 38).

Above all, use the activities in this book to add a sense of fun to your classroom. Varying the types of activities in which your students are engaged keeps their school days interesting, challenging, and fun. And a classroom in which students enjoy themselves is a classroom where learning is taking place.

State Shapes

Tap into your students' artistic intelligence by having them incorporate the shape of your state into a work of art.

Materials

• copy of the template on page 7, after you've added the state outline (see Getting Started, below)
• copies of your state's outline map (pages 62–64), copied at various sizes
• markers and colored pencils

Getting Started

Cut and paste your state's outline map into the top right-hand corner of the State Shapes template (page 7). Add a label for the state's name in the box. (See completed example, right.) Make a copy of this template for each student. I try to provide students with a page that has outline maps of their state in various sizes on it.

How-Tos

1. Tell students to rotate the map outlines, trying to visualize a picture that could be drawn that incorporates the outline.

2. Once they've conceptualized a picture, tell them to place the outline behind the template so that the outline is in the orientation in which it will be used in their picture. Have them hold the template up to a window and trace the outline onto the template, using a thick black marker.

3. Using markers or colored pencils, students should draw a fully realized picture that incorporates the outline of your state. Tell your students that they should not leave any white space in the picture. This forces them to visualize an entire scene, rather than just having an object floating in a sea of white space.

☆ TEACHER TIP

If you want to fully integrate your state unit across the curriculum, you might consider asking the art teacher to conduct this lesson.

SPECTACULAR

State Report Projects

for Any State

By Michael Gravois

SCHOLASTIC

PROFESSIONAL BOOKS

New York • Toronto • London • Auckland • Sydney
Mexico City • New Delhi • Hong Kong • Buenos Aires

Dedication

To the states in which I've lived, and to the
people who made my time there special—
Louisiana, New York, New Jersey,
Mississippi, and Tennessee.

Cover design by James Sarfati
Cover photos by Donnelley Marks
Interior design by Sydney Wright
Interior illustration by Teresa Anderko

ISBN 0-439-20573-5

Printed in the U.S.A.

Table of Contents

State Shapes

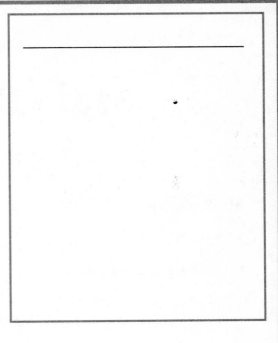

State Scavenger Hunt

Turn your students into explorers and archeologists by having them dig up a variety of items that represent your state.

Materials

• copy of the scavenger hunt list on page 9

Getting Started

I introduce this activity to my students on the first day of our Studying Our State unit. Give a copy of the scavenger hunt list on page 9 to each student.

How-Tos

1. Divide the class into groups of four or five. Tell students that they are to try to find as many items on the list as possible, and that they will be bringing them in to class on the last day of the unit.

2. Allow the groups twenty or thirty minutes to review the list. They should discuss which items group members already have and plan strategies for obtaining the hard-to-find items.

3. As they find objects, students should check it off the group list. (The student who has obtained the object could initial that item on the list, indicating that he or she will bring it in on the assigned day.)

4. I hold a culminating party in my class where we make State Cookies (see page 29). During this party each group presents the items from the list that it was able to find. Group members hold up each object for the class to see. They explain what the object is and where they found it. The group that finds the most objects from the list wins.

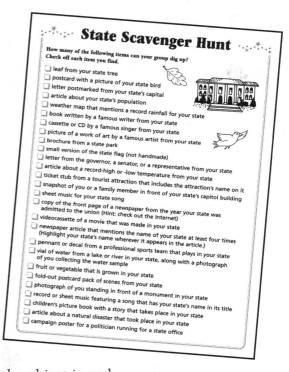

State Scavenger Hunt

How many of the following items can your group dig up? Check off each item you find.

- ☐ leaf from your state tree
- ☐ postcard with a picture of your state bird
- ☐ letter postmarked from your state's capital
- ☐ article about your state's population
- ☐ weather map that mentions a record rainfall for your state
- ☐ book written by a famous writer from your state
- ☐ cassette or CD by a famous singer from your state
- ☐ picture of a work of art by a famous artist from your state
- ☐ brochure from a state park
- ☐ small version of the state flag (not handmade)
- ☐ letter from the governor, a senator, or a representative from your state
- ☐ article about a record-high or -low temperature from your state
- ☐ ticket stub from a tourist attraction that includes the attraction's name on it
- ☐ snapshot of you or a family member in front of your state's capitol building
- ☐ sheet music for your state song
- ☐ copy of the front page of a newspaper from the year your state was admitted to the union (Hint: check out the Internet)
- ☐ videocassette of a movie that was made in your state
- ☐ newspaper article that mentions the name of your state at least four times (Highlight your state's name wherever it appears in the article.)
- ☐ pennant or decal from a professional sports team that plays in your state
- ☐ vial of water from a lake or river in your state, along with a photograph of you collecting the water sample
- ☐ fruit or vegetable that is grown in your state
- ☐ fold-out postcard pack of scenes from your state
- ☐ photograph of you standing in front of a monument in your state
- ☐ record or sheet music featuring a song that has your state's name in its title
- ☐ children's picture book with a story that takes place in your state
- ☐ article about a natural disaster that took place in your state
- ☐ campaign poster for a politician running for a state office

☆TEACHER TIP

You might also ask some parents to make foods representative of your state that can be served at your culminating party.

State Scavenger Hunt

How many of the following items can your group dig up?
Check off each item you find.

- ☐ leaf from your state tree
- ☐ postcard with a picture of your state bird
- ☐ letter postmarked from your state's capital
- ☐ article about your state's population
- ☐ weather map that mentions a record rainfall for your state
- ☐ book written by a famous writer from your state
- ☐ cassette or CD by a famous singer from your state
- ☐ picture of a work of art by a famous artist from your state
- ☐ brochure from a state park
- ☐ small version of the state flag (not handmade)
- ☐ letter from the governor, a senator, or a representative from your state
- ☐ article about a record-high or -low temperature from your state
- ☐ ticket stub from a tourist attraction that includes the attraction's name on it
- ☐ snapshot of you or a family member in front of your state's capitol building
- ☐ sheet music for your state song
- ☐ copy of the front page of a newspaper from the year your state was admitted to the union (Hint: check out the Internet)
- ☐ videocassette of a movie that was made in your state
- ☐ newspaper article that mentions the name of your state at least four times (Highlight your state's name wherever it appears in the article.)
- ☐ pennant or decal from a professional sports team that plays in your state
- ☐ vial of water from a lake or river in your state, along with a photograph of you collecting the water sample
- ☐ fruit or vegetable that is grown in your state
- ☐ fold-out postcard pack of scenes from your state
- ☐ photograph of you standing in front of a monument in your state
- ☐ record or sheet music featuring a song that has your state's name in its title
- ☐ children's picture book with a story that takes place in your state
- ☐ article about a natural disaster that took place in your state
- ☐ campaign poster for a politician running for a state office

ABC Charts

Creating ABC Charts will compel your students to learn a wide range of interesting facts about your state. A bulletin board featuring these charts will become a veritable information center.

Materials

• copy of page 11 for each student • markers and colored pencils

Getting Started

Students should write the alphabet down the left-hand side of a loose-leaf paper. They should then brainstorm a list of as many things related to their state as possible that begin with each letter of the alphabet. (A good way to get started is by looking through the index of a book about the state. Students can also flip through the book, reading captions, headlines, and italicized information.)

How-Tos

1. Once students have brainstormed their alphabetical lists, give each of them a copy of the template on page 11. Students should use their lists to pick one item for each letter that describes an interesting aspect of their state and write an alliterative phrase about it.

For example, next to the letters Aa on the template, they should write an alliterative phrase that describes the item from their list that begins with the letter A. (Such as "Awesome Astrodome" or "Astonishing Aspens.") They should do the same for each of the other letters of the alphabet.

2. In each square above the alliterative phrase, they should draw and color a picture that represents the concept.

3. On the back of the ABC Charts, students can write two sentences describing their illustrations.

4. After students have completed their ABC Charts, hang them on a bulletin board under a banner that reads, for example, "The ABCs of Texas" or "Texas Information Center."

Aa Bb Cc Dd Ee Ff
Gg Hh Ii Jj Kk Ll
Mm Nn Oo Pp Qq Rr
Ss Tt Uu Vv Ww Xx
Yy Zz

Landforms & Bodies of Water
Postcard Packs

Students can work individually or in groups as they learn about the landforms and bodies of water located in your state.

Materials

- manila file folder • white construction paper
- scissors • tape • markers and colored pencils

Getting Started

If students work individually, they can each create three postcards for their pack. To make this activity go a little faster, have students work in groups of four to six. Each group member can create one postcard for a group pack. (One student can be in charge of creating the case for the postcard pack.)

How-Tos

(These directions are for students working individually to create a postcard pack of three postcards. Adapt them if you want the students to work in groups.)

1. Each student should cut a sheet of white construction paper in half horizontally.

2. They should place the strips side by side to form one long strip, and then tape the two strips together. Have them fold the strip accordion style into four sections.

3. Tell students to measure the size of one of the postcards and then cut out a cover for the postcard pack from the folded edge of a manila file folder. This will serve as the case into which the postcards will be inserted. (You should be able to get two covers from each folder.)

① Cut here

② Tape

③

4. Have students open the folded paper and place it on their desks so that it forms two peaks (like the letter *M*).

   They should use a glue stick to attach the far-left rectangle to the underside of the manila cover. This leaves three postcards that fall out of the manila cover.

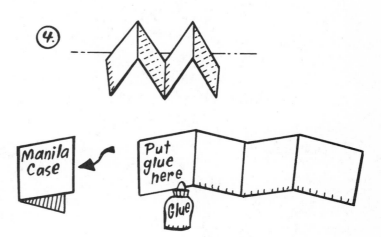

5. Have students choose three landforms or important bodies of water located in your state and create a colorful postcard for each. (See sample for the state of Louisiana on page 12.)

   On the back of each postcard, they should write a paragraph to the class that describes and defines the landform or body of water. The postcards can be addressed to the class, and students can create a stamp that is reflective of the geography of their state.

6. Finally, have them design an illustration for the cover of their postcard pack.

Famous People in History Posters

Add a bit of dramatic flair to your classroom as your students pretend to be historical personalities who helped your state become the rich, diverse place it is today.

Materials

• poster board • markers • scissors
• various craft materials (yarn, buttons, cotton)

Getting Started

People posters are a wonderful way to introduce the concept of first-person narratives to your class. After my students research their historical figures and create a poster of them, they give an oral report about that person to the class, speaking in the first person.

How-Tos

1. Tell students they will research a different historical figure from your state's past and create a people poster for that person. They will also present a short two-to-three-minute presentation about him or her.

2. Give each student a large sheet of poster board to create a people poster of the figure they chose. Students should cut

☆TEACHER TIP

I have my students bring in a prop that is representative of the historical figure and have them hold the prop during the presentation.

three holes in it: one for the face and two for the arms. The armholes should be at shoulder height. Have them draw the person's body, clothing, and hair on the poster board. They should also add a background and write the name of the person being represented across the top of the poster.

3. Students can use craft materials to give the poster some depth (e.g., yarn for hair, buttons for clothing, cotton for clouds in the background.)

4. During the oral reports, students should stick their arms through the armholes and place their face in the head hole. They should speak in the first person as if they were the historical figure.

After the report, open the floor up for questions. The class should ask questions as if they were speaking directly to the historical personality, addressing him or her by name.

5. Consider having a State History Party where the students wear their people posters and interact with one another as if they were all the historical figures on which they reported. Improvise a short scene that might take place if two characters were to meet.

Economy Quilts

A classroom wall or bulletin board will become a work of art
as your students piece together their quilt blocks featuring images
of things that make your state's economy flourish.

Materials

• template on page 17 • ruler • markers and colored pencils

Getting Started

Students should use an encyclopedia, almanacs, and other reference books, as well as the Internet
to research their state's economy. Have them list materials, goods, industries, and services that
bring money into your state.

How-Tos

1. Give each student a copy of
the template on page 17.

2. Ask them to choose eight
items from the list they
created about your state's
economy. For each of the
items, they should create a
repeating pattern that they
will draw and color in one
of the eight areas on the
construction paper. The
pattern will look like a
cloth swatch.

3. After the eight areas are
drawn and colored, hang
each of the quilt blocks next
to one another on a class wall or bulletin board so that the edges abut one another. This will
make it look as if there is a large quilt hanging on the wall.

4. As an extension activity, you can have students write eight short paragraphs that describe the
eight items they chose to illustrate on their quilt block. The paragraphs can be glued onto the
back of their artwork.

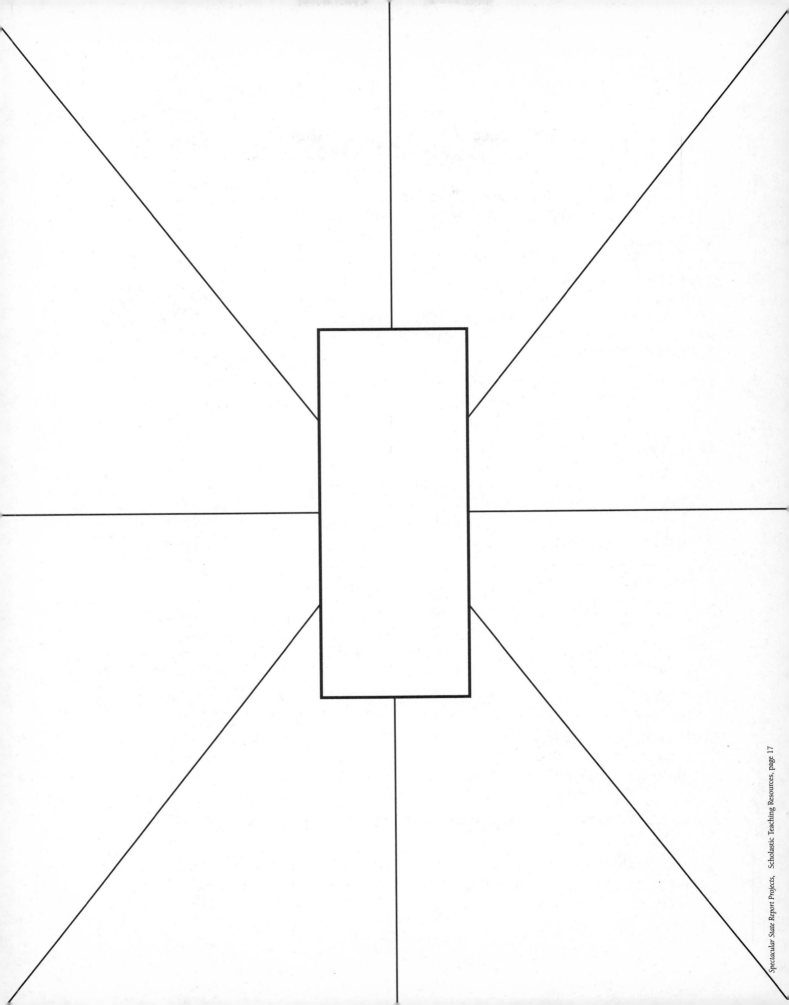

Film Scrolls From the Past

Your students will become photojournalists from the past as they document important events that helped shape the beginnings of your state.

Materials

• one tube from a paper towel roll per student • drinking straws
• white construction paper • copies of page 19 • colored pencils
or markers • tape • Exacto knife (for teacher use only) or scissors

Getting Started

Have your students bring in cardboard tubes from paper towel rolls.
Have students cut the roll in half. You may want to precut 4" x 1/4" slots in one
of each student's rolls using the Exacto knife.

How-Tos

1. Next, they should cover each roll with white construction paper. Have them
extend the construction paper a half inch beyond the ends of the roll and
then cut several slits in so they can fold the paper into the inside
of the rolls. Have them tape the paper to the inside of the rolls.

2. Give each student a copy of the template on page 19. Have
them follow the directions to create a six-panel roll of film.

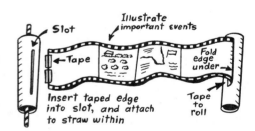

3. Students should choose six important moments from your
state's history to illustrate. (The events will be drawn in
chronological order from right to left, starting with panel one.)
Have them add an explanatory sentence to each frame.

4. Students should bend the right-hand tab of their film roll backward and tape it to the paper roll that does not have the slot.

5. They should put a couple of pieces of tape on the left-hand tab and thread it through the slot
in the second roll. Have them tape this tab to a straw that has been inserted into the roll. The
straw will act as a lock, preventing the filmstrip from being pulled out of the slot. Students
can trim the straw so that only a half inch of straw sticks out from each side of the roll.

6. Show students how to twist the straw, pulling the filmstrip into the left-hand roll. This will pull
the two paper rolls together.

7. Students should use creative lettering to write the name of their state on the left-hand roll and
a sentence on the right-hand roll explaining what the roll of film contains. Demonstrate how
the right-hand roll can be pulled to reveal the state's history, one panel at a time.

Film Template

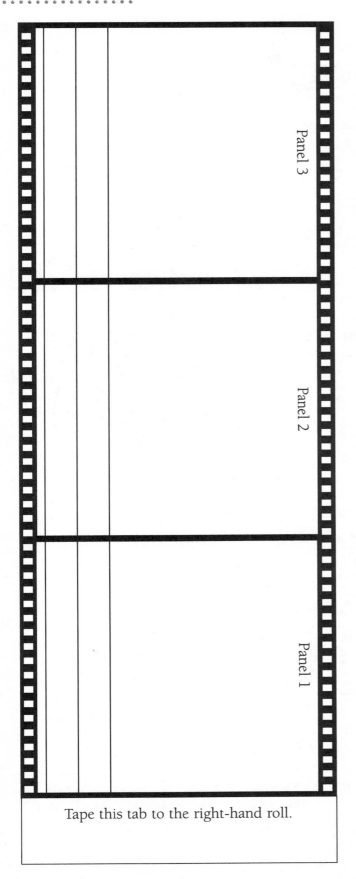

Panel 3

Panel 2

Panel 1

Tape this tab to the right-hand roll.

After you thread this tab through the slit in the left-hand roll, tape it to a straw.

Panel 6

Panel 5

Panel 4

TAB A: Glue this tab behind panel 3.

3-D Graphs

Incorporate mathematics into the study of your state by having your students create 3-D graphs comparing the populations of major cities or by tracing the population changes for the city or state in which you live.

Materials

- copy of the template on page 21 • construction paper
- scissors • glue sticks • markers and colored pencils

Getting Started

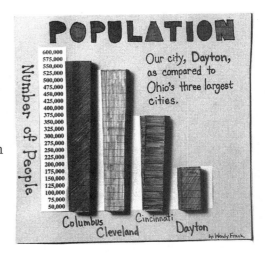

Decide what population statistics your students will be comparing. For example, they can compare the populations of major cities within your state, population changes for the city in which you live, population changes for your state since its admission into the union, populations of neighboring states, and so on. Give each student a copy of the graph template on page 21 and a sheet of construction paper. You may want to model how to make the graph before asking students to make one.

How-Tos

1. Ask students to write the population figures along the left-hand column of the graph.

2. They should decide what each column represents and shade the columns with markers or colored pencils up to the appropriate graph line.

3. Have them cut the graph out. They should cut away the unshaded top of each column.

4. Then they need to carefully fold the graph so that the columns stand out from the gray strips. A side view of the folded paper should look like this:

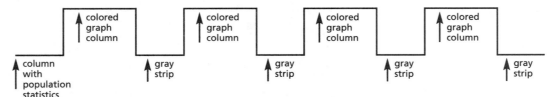

5. Students should use a glue stick to attach the gray strips to a piece of light-colored construction paper.

6. Finally, they should add headings down the left side and bottom of the graph that explain what the numbers and columns represent. They should also add a title.

3-D Graphs

Name _____

The numbers representing the populations you are comparing should be written next to the lines in this shaded column.

- Use colored pencils or markers to shade in the columns for the populations you are comparing.
- Cut the graph out and fold it into a 3-D graph following your teacher's instructions.
- Glue the 3-D graph onto a sheet of construction paper.
- Add the proper headings along the left side and bottom of the graph.
- Add a title to your graph.

State Riddle Books

Students can stump their classmates after they create these books that ask questions about interesting people, places, and things from your state.

Materials

• two copies of the template on page 23 for each student • colored markers and pencils • scissors • colored construction paper • glue sticks

Getting Started

Gather a variety of books about your state from which students can find interesting facts and information.

How-Tos

1. Give each student two copies of the template on page 23. Tell them to cut out the six riddle books.

2. They should place the books in front of them with the writing faceup. Have them fold the small bottom strip upward along the solid line and crease it. Then they should fold the top panel down, tuck it under the lower strip, and crease it.

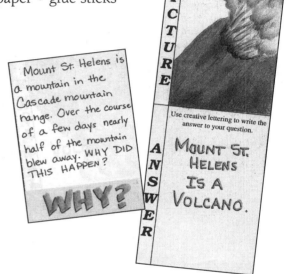

3. Students should write the following words on the small lower panels of the six riddle books, one word for each book—Who, What, When, Where, Why, and How. (See sample above.)

4. Tell students to use the information they found to write six questions relating to the 5W's and How.

5. On the cover of each book, they should list facts about the topic and ask a related question. For example, on the "What?" book, they could write the following: "I am as high as a 46-story building and contain enough concrete to build a two-lane highway from New York to Seattle. I am the greatest source of water power in the United States. What Am I?" (Answer: The Grand Coulee Dam) They should write other facts/questions on each of the other riddle books.

6. On the lower panel inside the riddle book, students should use creative lettering to write the answer to the question they posed on the cover. On the top panel inside the riddle book, they should draw a picture that illustrates the answer.

7. After the six riddle books are finished, students should use a glue stick to attach them to a sheet of colored construction paper. They should label the sheet, "The 5W's and How of (My State)." Hang the finished riddle books on a bulletin board so other students can quiz themselves.

State Riddle Books

- Cut out each riddle book along the dashed lines. This sheet produces three riddle books.
- On each riddle book, fold the small bottom panel up along the solid line.
- Fold the top panel down and tuck it behind the bottom panel.
- Follow your teacher's directions for completing each riddle book.

ANSWER

PICTURE

Use creative lettering to write the answer to your question.

Draw and color a picture that illustrates your question and answer.

(fold up here)

ANSWER

PICTURE

Use creative lettering to write the answer to your question.

Draw and color a picture that illustrates your question and answer.

(fold up here)

ANSWER

PICTURE

Use creative lettering to write the answer to your question.

Draw and color a picture that illustrates your question and answer.

(fold up here)

State Coat of Arms

Create an intriguing 3-D bulletin board featuring state coat of arms that illustrate the colorful history of your state.

Materials

- one copy of the State Coat of Arms template on page 25 for each student
- scissors • colored pencils • tape • white construction paper

Getting Started

Explain to the class the significance of a family coat of arms, mentioning that the objects on it reflect important aspects of the family's history. Ask if any of your students are familiar with their family's coat of arms, and if they know what the objects on it signify. Show examples if possible.

Students should also read information about your state's history—historical figures, indigenous people, important sites, economic factors, reasons for its formation, significant events, and so on.

How-Tos

1. Give each student a copy of the template on page 25 and a sheet of white construction paper.

2. After gathering information about your state's history, students should choose four key events to write about and illustrate. In each of the quadrants on the template, students should draw a detailed picture that represents the historical subject they chose.

3. Then, on the white construction paper, they should draw an icon to represent each quadrant. Next to each icon they should write a paragraph that describes the historical significance of each of the illustrations.

4. They should curl the top and bottom of the construction paper forward and backward respectively, so that it looks like a scroll. They can tape the curled paper into place.

   Next, they should cut out their state coat of arms. For durability, you might have them first glue it onto a sheet of construction paper before cutting it out.

5. Fold the two tabs back so they bend behind the coat of arms. Tape each tab so that when you attach the coat of arms to the bulletin board, they curve outward, creating a 3-D effect. Tape the scrolls next to each coat of arms.

State Coat of Arms Template

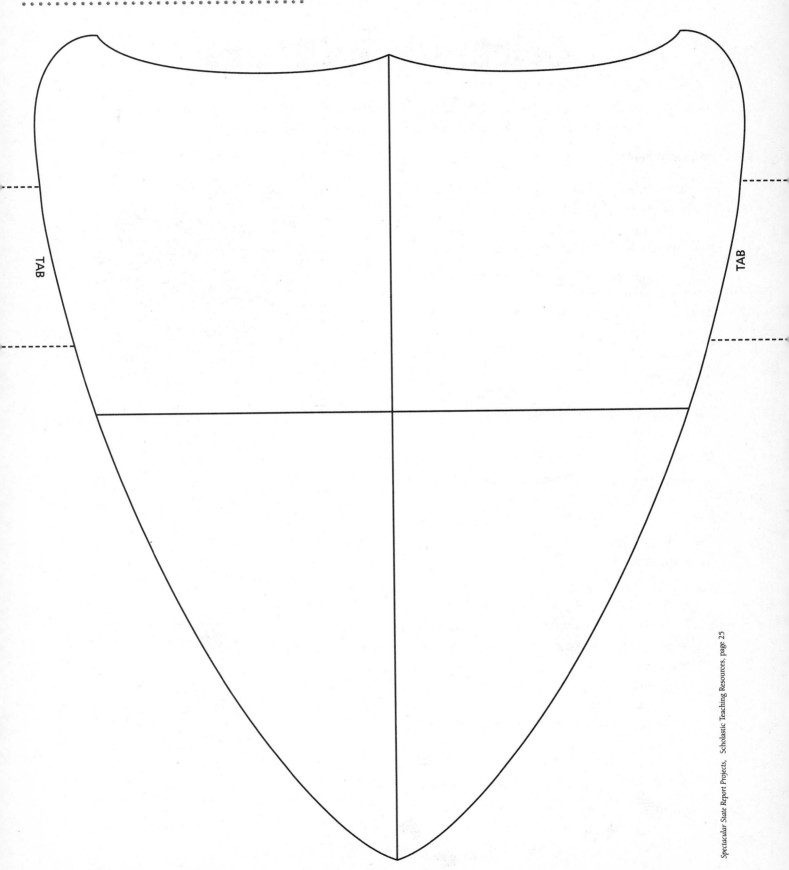

TAB

TAB

Celebrity Spinners

Put a unique spin on learning about famous people from your state by having your students create celebrity spinners.

Materials

- one manila folder per student • glue sticks
- thread • copies of the circles template on page 28
- colored pencils or markers • tape • ruler • pencil
- Exacto knife (for teacher's use only) or scissors

Getting Started

Depending on the grade level you're teaching, you may want to cut out the disks using an Exacto knife prior to beginning this activity.

How-Tos

1. Give each student a manila folder and a copy of the template on page 28.

2. Students should use a pencil and ruler to draw a line six inches from the folded edge of the manila folder. They should then cut along this line, cutting through both sides of the manila folder.

3. Have the students cut out the two circles on the circle template.

4. Students should place Circle Number 1 in the center of the manila folder and trace around it with a pencil. Using scissors (or the teacher or parent can use an Exacto knife), students should cut the circle out of both sides on the manila folder. They should cut the circle out as carefully as possible, as they will be using both the circle and the manila folder to complete this activity. You should have them cut the circle out of one side of the manila folder, and then have them trace around the hole they just cut to create an exact duplicate of that circle on the other half of the manila folder. They can then cut the second circle out.

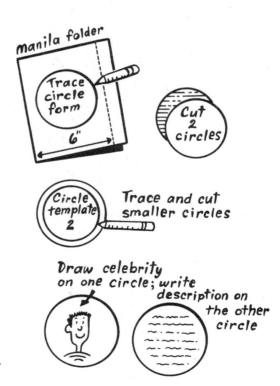

The two circles that students cut out of the folder will now have to be made a little smaller. Students should take Circle Number 2 from the template and place it on top of each circle. They should trace around the template and cut it out. They will now have two manila circles that are a little smaller than the circular holes that they cut out of the folder.

5. On one of the manila circles, students should draw a picture of a famous person from their state. The person should be in a scene or in a pose that reflects his or her significance.

On the other circle, students should write a descriptive paragraph that details the importance of the person on whom they chose to report.

6. Give each student a seven-inch piece of thread. Have students tape the thread vertically behind the illustration of the famous person so that an equal amount of the thread is above and below the circle.

Students should glue the two circles together—back-to-back—with the thread running vertically between them, creating a spinning disk.

7. Students should cut a small slit in the folded edge of the manila folder, directly below the circular hole.

They should feed the thread through this hole so that the spinner is set in the exact center of the hole. They can tape the thread to the back of the manila folder. Students should pull the other end of the thread taut and tape this piece of thread to the back of the manila folder as well.

8. They should then use a glue stick to seal the folder. The spinner should now hang freely and turn within the hole.

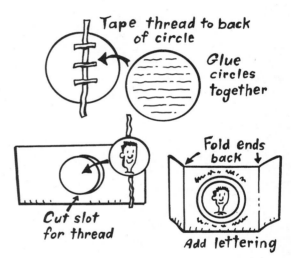

9. Above the spinner, students should use creative lettering to write the name of the famous person. Below the spinner, they should write a phrase describing the person.

10. Students should bend the right and left edges of the folder backward (about two inches on each side) so that the folder can stand on its own, allowing the spinner to turn.

11. Line the spinners up on a shelf or table to create an animated display of people who made significant contributions to your state.

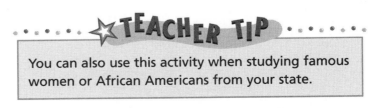

★TEACHER TIP

You can also use this activity when studying famous women or African Americans from your state.

Spinner Template

Circle Number 1
Use the template to cut two
circles out of your folder.

Circle Number 2
Use this template to make
the two smaller circles.

State Cookies

Making cookies in the shape of your state is a fun and delicious way to discuss important topographical features of your state with your class.

Materials

• topographical map of your state • oak tag • knife • oven

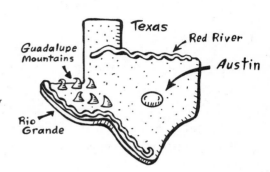

This activity can be done whenever you discuss the topographical features of your state, but I do this on the last day of our unit as a fun way to celebrate all that we've learned.

How-Tos

The following recipe will make about 20 four-inch cookies. Adjust according to your class size.

• 1/2 C white or brown sugar	• 1/2 C butter	• 2 eggs
• 2 1/2 C flour	• 2 tsps. baking powder	• 1 tsp. vanilla
• blue icing	• white icing	
• decorations such as sprinkles (different colors depending on the topographical features of your state), chocolate chips, and M&M's		

1. Cream sugar and butter together. Beat in the eggs, flour, baking powder, and vanilla. Chill the dough for three or four hours before rolling. (We make the dough in the morning and bake the cookies after lunch.)

2. While the dough is chilling, each student should trace an outline of the state onto a piece of oak tag. Students then cut out the outline to use as a template to make the cookies.

3. Preheat the oven to 375°. Roll out the dough and cut it into four-inch squares. Give one to each student.

4. Have students place their oak tag template over the dough and use a butter knife to cut out their state. (I let them use their extra dough to make a small cookie.)

5. Discuss the topographical features of your state with students. As you discuss certain features, let students add them to their cookies. For example, they can use chocolate chips for mountain ranges, kisses for larger mountains, red hots for volcanoes, green sprinkles for grasslands or swamps, and M&M's for the capital and major cities. Tell them to add other things, like icing, to show features such as rivers after they've baked the cookies.

6. Place cookies on a greased cookie sheet and bake for 10–11 minutes.

Learning About Our Region

Working within cooperative groups allows for social engagement in learning. Invite students to work with their classmates as they create Learning Posters about the other states in their region of the country.

Materials

• five-foot strips of bulletin board paper for each group • construction paper • colored markers and pencils • scissors • one copy of the graph template on page 21 for each group • one index card per student • two copies of the circle book template on page 32 for each group • one copy of the Learning About Our Region requirement sheet on page 31 for each student • one copy of the snapshot template on page 33 for every two students • books about your region

Getting Started

Divide your class into as many groups as there are states in your region. Tell students that each group will create a Learning Poster for one of these states. Give each group a five-foot section of bulletin board paper. I use different color paper for each group.

How-Tos

1. Give each student a copy of the Learning About Our Region requirement sheet on page 31. Review it with the class. Tell them that it will be up to each group to decide which group member will be responsible for completing each element of the Learning Poster. Stress that part of their final grade will be determined by how well they share the production of the final poster.

Tell them that all group members should proofread everything on the poster, regardless of who created each element. Spelling will count as part of their final grade.

2. Pass out one copy of the graph template (page 21), one copy of the snapshot template (page 33) for every two students, an index card for every student, and two copies of the circle book template (page 32) to each group.

3. After the Learning Posters are completed, hang them up in the hall so that other classes can learn about the states in their region.

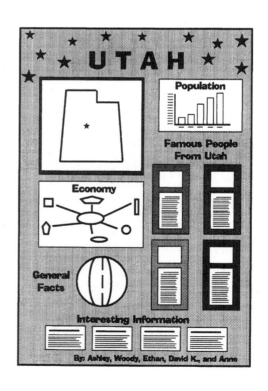

Learning About Our Region

Requirement Sheet

☐ **Title**
Write the name of the state and region in large letters across the top of your poster. List the names of each group member beneath the title.

☐ **Map**
Draw a detailed map of your state and its neighbors. Include pertinent information on the map such as a scale, a key, capital cities and major cities, landforms, rivers, lakes, and a compass rose. Attach this map to your poster under the main title.

☐ **Graphic Organizer**
Create a graphic organizer that presents information about your state's economy. Attach the graphic organizer to your poster under the title "Economy."

☐ **Graph**
Use the 3-D graph template to highlight the populations of your state's four largest cities. Attach the graph to your poster under the title "Population."

☐ **Circle Book**
Use the Circle Book template to report on the state bird, tree, flower, and nickname.

Each page of the Circle Book should include a small illustration in the space at the top, and a few sentences about the topic written on the lines at the bottom.

Follow the instructions on the template to construct the circle book, and then attach it to your poster under the title "General Facts."

☐ **Famous People**
Use the snapshot template to draw a famous historical figure from your state's past. Beneath the drawing, write a brief biography of the historical figure explaining his or her significance. Attach the template to your poster under the title "Famous People."

☐ **Interesting Information**
Each person in the group should choose one interesting fact about his or her state and write a detailed paragraph about it on an index card. Attach the index cards to the poster under the title "Interesting Information."

Circle Book Template

Creating a Circle Book

1. Fold each circle in half.

2. Use a glue stick to attach the backs of side one and side two.

3. Attach the backs of side two and side three, and side three and side four.

4. Glue the backs of the first and last sides directly to the poster so the four pages can be turned like the pages of a book.

Snapshot Template

Use this template to write a complete, detailed paragraph about a famous person from the state you are researching. Draw a picture of the person in the snapshot frame. Fill the entire frame with color. Write a title for your paragraph on the top line. Cut out the template and attach it to your group's learning poster.

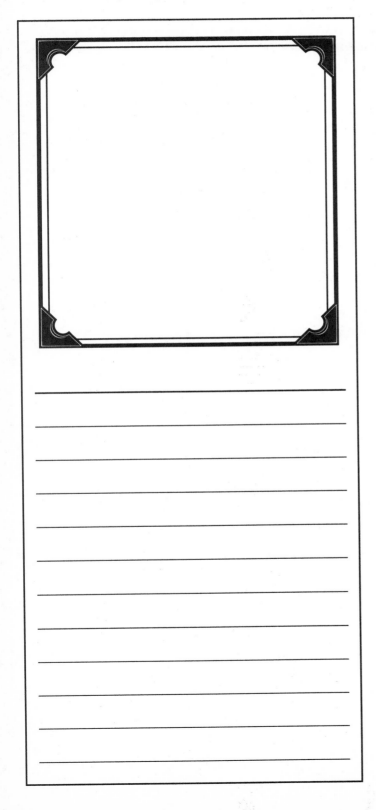

State Facts Domino Books

As your students enter information into their Domino Books, they will learn about the flora, fauna, minerals, and symbols that were chosen to represent your state.

Materials

• colored construction paper • scissors • rulers • markers and colored pencils • copies of the templates on pages 35–36

Getting Started

Decide how long you want the Domino Books to be. The How-Tos are for a nine-panel Domino Book. The book will include panels featuring the state flag, bird, flower, tree, animal, gem, fish, and nickname. If you want your Domino Book to be longer, you will need to decide on what additional information you want your students to include.

How-Tos

1. Give each student two sheets of colored construction paper. Tell them to cut each sheet of construction paper in half vertically. Each student will use three of these strips. (This means you'll need three sheets of construction paper for every pair of students.)

2. Students should place the three strips next to each other horizontally as shown and tape the edges, forming one long strip.

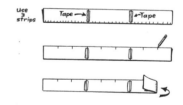

3. Students should use a ruler to divide each strip into thirds, placing a small tick mark to indicate where each third is. Tell them to fold the far right edge inward, creasing the paper along the first tick mark. They will continue to fold the paper inward, creasing along each tick mark. The Domino Book will be folded into nine panels.

The top panel will serve as the cover. (This panel should open out toward the left, like the cover of a book.) On the cover, students should create a title panel for their Domino Book.

4. When students open the cover, it will reveal two panels. On the left panel they should glue the snapshot frame for the state flag. Have them illustrate the flag. On the right panel (which is actually the back of panel three), they should write the title "State Flag" and a paragraph about the flag.

5. Have students open the Domino Book to the next panel. They should glue their next snapshot on the left panel, illustrate it, and write the title and description on the right panel. (They can put the frames in any order they wish.)

They should continue doing this until all eight panels have a snapshot on them. The ninth interior panel (a right-hand panel) will include the paragraph that describes the snapshot on panel eight.

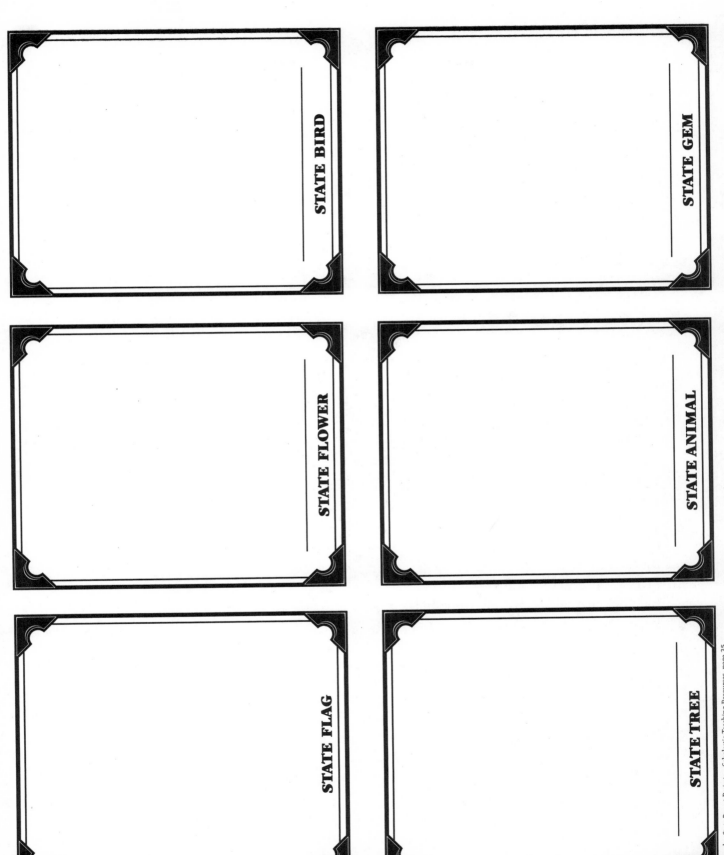

STATE BIRD

STATE GEM

STATE FLOWER

STATE ANIMAL

STATE FLAG

STATE TREE

STATE NICKNAME

STATE FISH

Three-Step Travel Guides

This creative Travel Guide adds a unique visual twist
to the standard trifold brochure format.

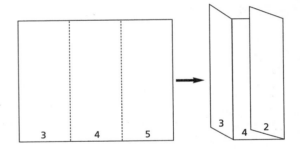

Materials

• white construction paper • scissors • markers and colored pencils

Getting Started

I've included the requirements that I assigned to my fifth-graders.
Adjust them as you see fit.

How-Tos

1. Have students fold the construction paper into thirds as shown. The left panel should overlap the right panel. (The front cover will be called "panel 1;" the top of the right panel will be called "panel 2;" and the three interior panels will be called "panels 3, 4, and 5.")

2. Tell students panel 1 should include a title, an outline of the state, and an enticing slogan to get people to visit the state. At the top of panel, students should draw a landform that is unique to the state. The uppermost point of the landform should be about one and a half to two inches from the top of the panel. After drawing and coloring the cover, students should cut away the excess paper above the top of the landform.

3. On panel 2 students should draw a picture of a famous person so that his or her head and torso are at the right edge of panel 2. They should cut away the excess paper at the top left of the torso, cutting around the head as well. Tell them to write the person's name and a paragraph describing him or her.

4. Panel 3 has been cut in the shape of the landform that is on the cover. Students should hold panel 3 up to a classroom window and trace the landform from panel 1, and then color it. Below this drawing, students should write a paragraph describing the landform.

5. The top of panel 4 will feature the skyline of a major city in their state. The skyline should be at the very top of this panel and feature a few important buildings. The buildings should be labeled. Have students cut away the excess paper from above and between the buildings. Underneath the skyline have them write the name of the city and a short description of it.

6. Panel 5 is opposite the one featuring the famous person. On this panel, students should list some interesting facts about their state.

Ecology Circle Books

The phrase "Save Our Planet" sounds overwhelming. We think, What impact can one individual have on the planet? Focusing on one state's ecology helps students understand that if every state did its part we could, as a country, have an enormous impact on our planet's health.

Materials

- one copy of the templates on pages 43–49 for each student
- scissors • glue sticks • oak tag • colored markers
- materials for the two experiments (see page 40)

Getting Started

Creating the Ecology Circle Book will take several days to complete. My class usually creates one page per lesson, taking approximately two weeks to finish the project. The number of lessons your class completes will determine the project's time span.

My students have a Project Folder, in which they keep each of the completed pages until we are ready to construct the Circle Book.

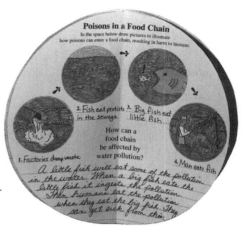

How-Tos

There are at least seven pages in the Ecology Circle Book. Below are directions for completing each page, followed by instructions for putting the Circle Book together and creating an attractive bulletin board.

Begin each lesson by passing out the Circle Book template that the class will complete that day.

Page 1: Ecology Vocabulary

1. Throughout the course of this activity, introduce the class to relevant terms. They should add each word and its definitions to this page as you discuss them.

2. You might consider writing the vocabulary words in bold letters on the template before copying them for your class.

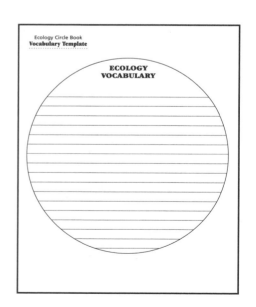

☆TEACHER TIP

Copy each template onto different colored paper to make the Circle Books more vibrant.

Then students can just add the definitions as the terms are explained. You can use more than one page if necessary. Determine how many lines should be left empty for the students to write the definition.

Vocabulary words could include: protists, ozone, ultraviolet rays, greenhouse effect, chlorofluorocarbons (CFCs), environmentalism, Environmental Protection Agency, pollutant, sewage, groundwater, carbon monoxide, scrubber, toxic wastes, landfill, recycle, reclamation, and noise pollution.

Page 2: Causes/Effects/Solutions

1. I talk about a number of ecological problems our state faces, and for each topic, we create a circle page. The number of pages your class completes will be determined by the number of issues you discuss.

2. On this page, your class should list the problem at the top of the page, using bold letters. Underneath the title, they should define the problem.

3. During the discussion, they should write the causes of the problem, its effects on the environment, and solutions to the problem. Since there is not a lot of room, they can write in sentence fragments.

4. Finally, they should choose one cause, one effect, and one solution for which they will draw an icon in the circles above each section.

Suggested topics of discussion could include: water pollution (freshwater and/or saltwater), garbage, smog, acid rain, ozone depletion, global warming, toxic waste pollution, deforestation, or energy overconsumption.

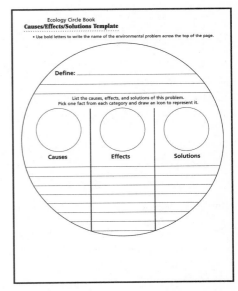

Page 3: Poisons in a Food Chain

1. Under the four circles, students should write a phrase describing the ways poisons enter the food chain and are ultimately consumed by humans.

The four steps might be 1) factory dumping 2) small fish eat protists in the sewage 3) big fish eat the small fish 4) people catch and eat the big fish

2. Students should draw thumbnail pictures illustrating these four steps.

3. On the lines at the bottom of the page, students should write a paragraph describing these steps in greater detail.

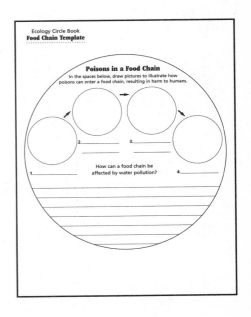

Page 4: Experiment—Observing Water Pollution

1. For this experiment you need six clear plastic glasses, a jug of water, and food coloring (red works well).

2. Fill the first glass with water and add a few drops of food coloring.

3. Explain that polluted water gets diluted as the water merges with other water sources. Illustrate this by pouring half of the polluted water into the second glass and filling it the rest of the way with clear water. Pour half of the water from cup #2 into cup #3, and add more clear water. Continue this process using all six cups. The water in cup #6 looks clear, but we know that some of the pollution still remains.

4. Students should answer the questions on the template after the experiment is completed. They should draw a picture of the experiment in the box at the top of the template.

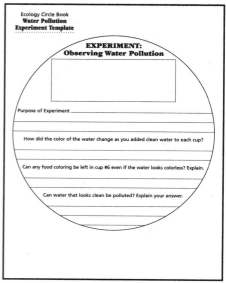

Page 5: Experiment—Observing Air Pollution

1. For this experiment, you need the lids from two jars, white construction paper, a glue stick, and some petroleum jelly. Use the lids to trace two circles onto the construction paper. Cut the circles out.

Glue each circle into the lids.

2. Rub some petroleum jelly onto the construction paper circles.

3. Place one of the lids outside in a place where it won't be disturbed, and place the other one inside the classroom.

4. Wait a couple of days and then check each lid for pollutants that stick to the petroleum jelly.

5. Students should answer the questions on the template and draw a picture of the experiment in the box at the top of the template.

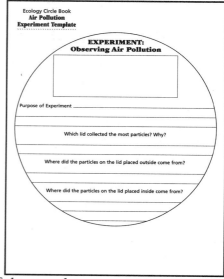

Page 6: Do You Know the Difference? Renewable and Nonrenewable Resources

1. Discuss the difference between renewable and nonrenewable resources.

Ask students for suggestions that fall into each category. They should list these under the

appropriate column as you write them on the board. Suggested responses include:

Renewable resources: wind energy, solar energy, geothermal energy, water energy, forests, wildlife

Nonrenewable resources: fossil fuels (for example, coal and oil), natural gas, copper, lead, minerals, soil

2. On the lines at the bottom of the template, have students write a paragraph describing the differences between these two types of resources.

Page 7: Do You Know the Difference? Recyclable and Nonrecyclable

1. Discuss the difference between materials that can and cannot be recycled.

Ask students for suggestions that fall into each category. List these under the appropriate column on the board.

Suggested responses include:

Things that can be recycled: paper products, glass, plastic, tin, copper, aluminum, cardboard, gold, wood, food, grass clippings, manure, tires, magnetic metal.

Things that cannot be recycled: crystal, light bulbs, milk-white class, nonmagnetic metal, waxed paper, plate glass.

2. On the lines at the bottom of the template, students should write a list of things that they can do to help make their state's environment a healthier one. They should use information they've collected throughout the course of this project.

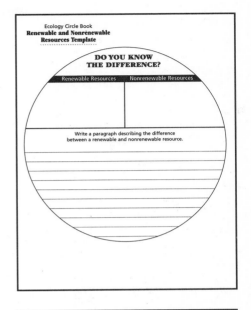

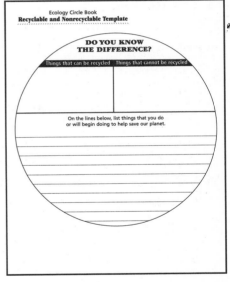

Creating the Circle Book

After all the pages are completed, students should cut out each circle. They should then follow the steps below to construct the interior pages of the Circle Book.

• Fold each circle in half.

• Use a glue stick to attach the right half of the back of side one to the left half of the back of side two.

• Attach the backs of side two and side three, and so on, in the same way.

• The backs of the first and last sides should not be glued together.

Students should place the first and last pages of the circle book on a sheet of oak tag and trace around them. Then they should cut out the oak tag circle. This will be used as the cover for the circle book.

They should use markers to create an attractive cover that includes a drawing and the title "Saving Our Planet . . . One State at a Time." They should also write their name on the cover. Have them then glue the first and last pages to the cover.

To reinforce the spine of the Circle Books, I have my students squirt a little liquid glue between the folded pages and the oak tag. As the glue dries, students should open each page so that they are not glued closed.

Creating the Bulletin Board

Create a banner that reads "SAVING THE PLANET . . . ONE STATE AT A TIME." Attach the banner to the bulletin board curving it outward a couple of times to create a 3-D effect.

Staple or tack the front and back covers of the Circle Books to the bulletin board so that the pages fan out, creating an interesting display.

Culminating Activity

At the end of this unit, I integrate the language arts skill of writing a formal letter. I have my students choose one of the problems plaguing our state's environment and write a letter to our state's governor asking him or her to address the issue. I put the students' letters in one big envelope and mail them to the governor. Our governor has responded each time, and my class is thrilled to receive an official response. At right is a letter we received from Governor Christie Todd Whitman when I was teaching in New Jersey.

CHRISTINE TODD WHITMAN
Governor

State of New Jersey
OFFICE OF THE GOVERNOR
CN-001
TRENTON NJ 08625-0001

The Fifth Grade Class
Wilson School
Westfield, New Jersey 07090

June 11, 1996

Dear Students:

Thank you for your letters. I am always delighted to hear from students who are concerned about the environment.

In New Jersey all of us must play a part in working to protect our environment and keep our world a safe and beautiful place in which to live. I think it is wonderful that you understand the importance of addressing environmental problems. Whether you participate in your local recycling program or ask others to dispose of litter properly, you can make a valuable contribution to your own future and to the future of New Jersey and the world.

The Department of Environmental Protection (DEP) has developed programs that involve citizen and student groups, such as "Water Watch" and "Adopt A Beach," two water-related programs in which participants study, monitor, and clean up a section of a stream, river, lake, or beach in their community. Another program is the "Litter-Acy Club," in which participants conduct recycling and other waste-reduction projects.

On April 27, I had the pleasure of joining concerned citizens in Sandy Hook for a "beach sweep" organized by the DEP in conjunction with several environmental groups. I have also adopted my own beach. For more information about this program you can call (609) 29-BEACH.

Additionally, the Clean Communities Program has been successful in stimulating public awareness of the State's cleanup efforts and teaching people about the harmful effects of litter and how to prevent them. While my budget proposal for Fiscal Year 1997 would transfer the grants portion of the program to the Department of Treasury, the program would continue to help municipalities and counties address this important issue.

The DEP has a Public Access Center that can provide you with the department's free publications. You can call the center at (609) 777-DEPS to request information on a variety of environmental subjects.

Again, thank you for writing, and best wishes for success in your studies.

Sincerely yours,

Christine Todd Whitman
Governor

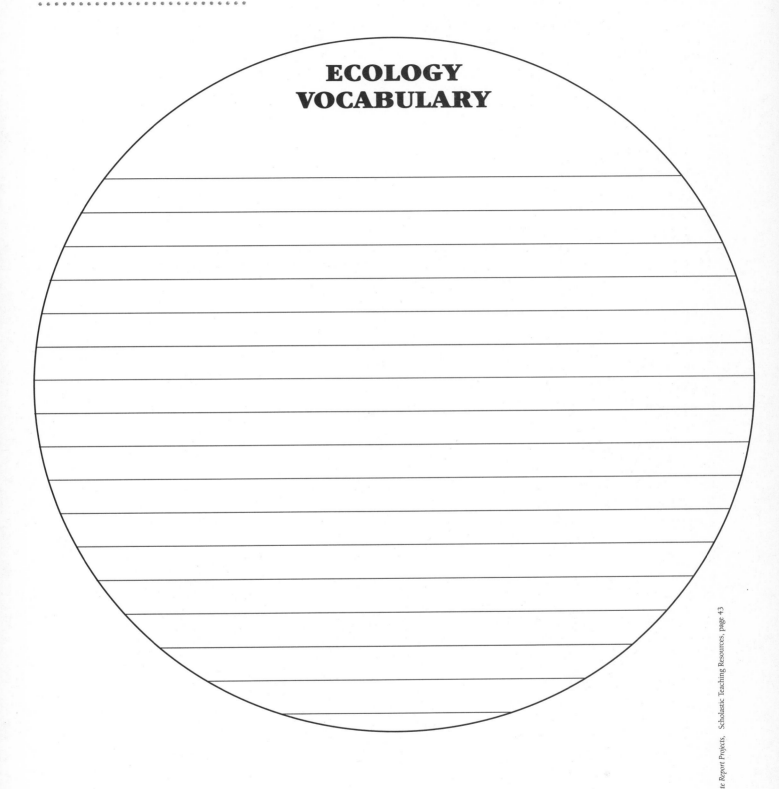

ECOLOGY VOCABULARY

Ecology Circle Book
Causes/Effects/Solutions Template

• Use bold letters to write the name of the environmental problem across the top of the page.

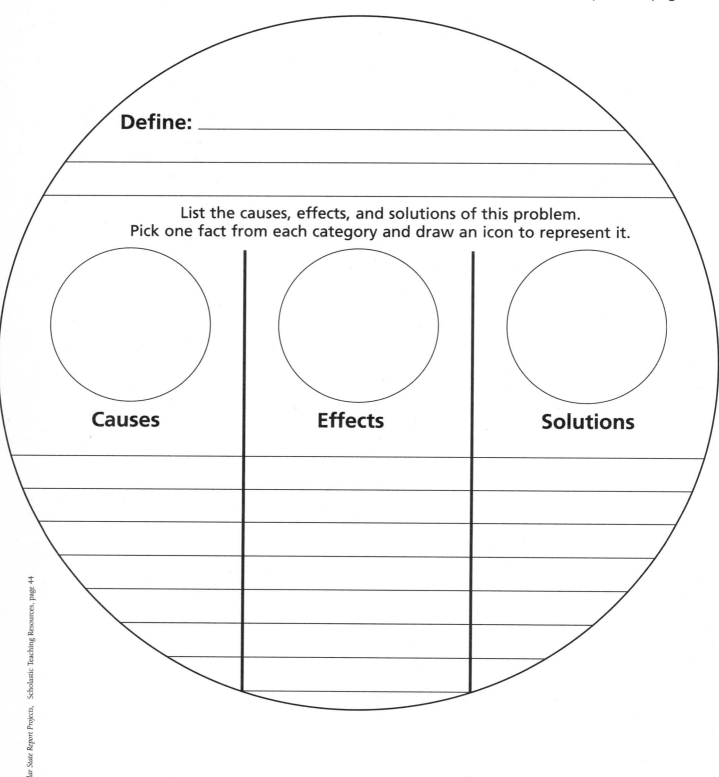

Define: _____

_____

_____

List the causes, effects, and solutions of this problem.
Pick one fact from each category and draw an icon to represent it.

Causes   **Effects**   **Solutions**

Poisons in a Food Chain

In the spaces below, draw pictures to illustrate how poisons can enter a food chain, resulting in harm to humans.

2._____

_____

3._____

How can a food chain be affected by water pollution?

1._____

4._____

Water Pollution
Experiment Template

EXPERIMENT:
Observing Water Pollution

Purpose of Experiment _____

How did the color of the water change as you added clean water to each cup?

Can any food coloring be left in cup #6 even if the water looks colorless? Explain.

Can water that looks clean be polluted? Explain your answer.

EXPERIMENT:
Observing Air Pollution

Purpose of Experiment _____

Which lid collected the most particles? Why?

Where did the particles on the lid placed outside come from?

Where did the particles on the lid placed inside come from?

Renewable and Nonrenewable
Resources Template

DO YOU KNOW
THE DIFFERENCE?

Renewable Resources	Nonrenewable Resources

Write a paragraph describing the difference
between a renewable and nonrenewable resource.

Recyclable and Nonrecyclable Template

DO YOU KNOW THE DIFFERENCE?

Things that can be recycled	Things that cannot be recycled

On the lines below, list things that you do
or will begin doing to help save our planet.

I Packed a Suitcase to . . .

Students will learn about the importance of tourism in your state by studying important places that attract tourists and by designing a visitor's suitcase.

Materials

• colored construction paper • scissors • glue sticks • markers and colored pencils

Getting Started

Gather tourist guides and brochures from local visitors' centers or from your state's department of tourism for your students to use as reference materials. Tell students that each of them should research three areas in your state that attract tourists. Explain that they will design a suitcase with three "compartments" that contain items a tourist would need to pack when visiting each site.

How-Tos

1. First, have students brainstorm a list of items a tourist might need when visiting each tourist site. Students can use creative license. For instance, if a tourist were to go white-water rafting, he or she might pack a rubber boat and paddles (even though these would not logically be packed in a suitcase).

2. Give each student one large and three small sheets of construction paper. Students should fold the three smaller sheets in half horizontally. These three sheets represent the three compartments of the suitcase.

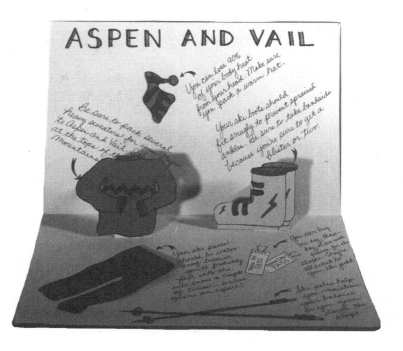

3. Next, students draw and cut out different articles of clothing, accessories, and items needed when visiting the site. (For example, if the tourist were visiting Aspen, Colorado, he or she might pack a hat, sweater, ski pants, ski poles, ski boots, and lift passes.) These items should be glued around the inside of the folded piece of construction paper.

4. Next to each item, students should write a description of the item and explain why each item is needed.

5. Students should repeat steps 3 and 4 for the other sites.

6. When the three compartments are finished, tell students to use a glue stick to attach the bottom of one compartment to the top side of the next, until the three pages are joined and turn like the pages in a book. (Use a glue stick instead of regular glue so the paper doesn't buckle.)

7. The large sheet of construction paper should be wrapped around the three compartments, cut to fit, and then glued around them.

8. Ask students to create a "sticker" that reads, "I Packed a Suitcase to (Name of State)" and glue it to the suitcase cover. (See the photograph on page 50.) Students should then create smaller stickers that feature the names of the tourist attractions.

9. Finally, students should fold a small rectangle of construction paper in half and cut out a handle for the suitcase. The bottom four tabs of the handle should be glued around the fold of the suitcase's covering.

Pop-Up Suitcases

For a more interesting and inventive suitcase, have the students follow the instructions on page 52 to create pop-up elements in each of the suitcase compartments. Be sure to model the process before asking students to do it themselves.

Creating Pop-Up Compartments
for the Suitcases

1. Fold a piece of construction paper in half horizontally.

2. To create each pop-up tab, cut two slits along the folded edge. Varying the lengths of the tabs will make the items in the compartment more three-dimensional.

3. Open the paper up, and gently pull each of the pop-up tabs forward.

4. Fold the paper again so that each of the pop-up tabs falls into the center. Make it crease at the base of each tab.

5. On a separate sheet of paper, draw the pop-up elements that will be "packed" in this compartment. Cut them out and glue them onto the front of each tab.

6. "Pack" other items into your compartment by gluing them below and above the pop-up items.

7. Use a pen to write a description of each item. Explain why it is important for a visitor to pack each item when visiting the tourist destination you chose.

8. Glue the bottom of one page to the top of the next, until all of the pages are joined. (Use a glue stick rather than glue so that the paper doesn't buckle. Be careful not to put glue where a tab on the opposite page will be or it will glue the tab closed and the page will rip.)

9. Make a cover for your suitcase by wrapping a large sheet of construction paper over the pop-up pages. Glue it into place.

Native American Trioramas

Creating trioramas about the first people who lived in your
state will make your state's history come alive for your students.

Materials

- copies of the graphic organizers on pages 55–56
- white construction paper (8 ½" x 14")
- stapler • colored construction paper
- markers and colored pencils • glue sticks
- scissors • various craft materials

Getting Started

Students can work individually or in pairs
for this activity. You should gather books
from local and school libraries that describe
the Indian groups in your state.

How-Tos

1. Pass out copies of the graphic organizers on pages 55–56 to each student (or pairs of students). Have them complete them using the resources you gathered.

2. Students will use the information from two of the categories on the graphic organizer to create two triorama displays. (See the instructions for creating the Trioramas on page 54.)

3. Provide construction paper, string, cotton, markers, craft sticks, and other materials so students can make the triorama scenes look as three-dimensional as possible.

4. On the bottom flap of each scene, students will write a complete, detailed paragraph describing the scene. They should use the information from their graphic organizers to help them write the paragraphs.

5. Glue the two trioramas together and then staple them onto a bulletin board. A small banner with the name of the featured Native American group can be stapled above each triorama display.

☆TEACHER TIP

You might consider having students work in groups of four, with each member being responsible for creating one scene. The four scenes can be glued side by side to form a four-sided pyramid display. The pyramids can be displayed on a table or countertop.

Creating the Trioramas

1. Fold the top left corner of the white construction paper diagonally so that the top edge of the paper is flush with the right edge of the paper.

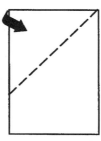

2. Fold the top right corner diagonally so that it touches the lower point of the previous fold.

3. Fold the rectangular panel at the bottom up so that a horizontal crease is made.

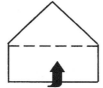

4. Open the paper up and cut the lower left diagonal crease. Cut it up to the center point of the paper.

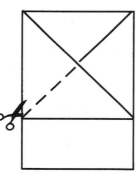

5. Repeat steps 1–4 so you can create two trioramas.

6. Choose two of the categories from your graphic organizers and create two scenes. Draw the background of your scenes across the upper and right-hand quadrants. The ground areas for each scene should be drawn on the left-hand quadrants.

7. For each triorama, pull point A over to point B so that the piece you just cut is flush with the lower right diagonal crease. This will form the triorama display. Glue the base into place.

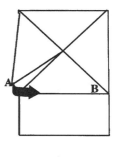

8. Use construction paper, string, cotton, markers, craft sticks, and other craft materials to make the scene look as three-dimensional as possible. Add a title banner across the top of the scene.

9. Use a ruler to lightly draw pencil lines on the bottom flap and write a complete, detailed paragraph describing each of the scenes you created. Erase the pencil lines after writing the paragraph.

10. When the two trioramas displays are finished, glue them side by side. From underneath tape the lower panels so that they form a corner.

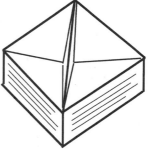

11. Staple the displays to the bulletin board. Create a small banner with the name of the featured Indian group and staple it above the trioramas.

Graphic Organizer 1

Fill out the graphic organizer as it relates to the Indian group you are researching. Below each drawing write facts about the topic that will help you write a paragraph about it.

INDIAN GROUP

Shelter

Draw a picture of their type of home.

Clothing

Draw a picture of their clothing.

Food

Draw a picture of some foods they ate.

Family Life

Draw a picture of an aspect of family life.

Graphic Organizer 2

Fill out the graphic organizer as it relates to the Indian group you are researching. Below each drawing write facts about the topic that will help you write a paragraph about it.

INDIAN GROUP

Art, Sculpture & Design

Draw a picture of a typical art style.

Political Structure

Draw a picture of the leader of this group.

Religious Life

Draw a picture of one of their ceremonies.

Topic of Your Choice

Draw a picture related to the topic you chose.

Papier-Mâché Zoos

Students are always thrilled to work with papier-mâché.
It's messy, but not too messy. It's creative, but not intimidating.
It's easy, but challenging. And best of all, it's fun.

Materials

- newspaper • masking tape • flour • salt • water
- plastic dish pans • paint • paint brushes
- a copy of the graphic organizer on page 59
- various craft materials (described below)
- clothes hanger • plastic grocery bags
- sandwich bags • cardboard tubes from
paper towel rolls

Getting Started

Because papier-mâché needs time to dry, as do the final coats of paint, this activity will take several days.

Before beginning the activity, research and discuss the various animals that are indigenous to your state. Each student should pick an animal that he or she will create out of papier-mâché. Students can work individually, in pairs, or in groups. However, if they are working in pairs or groups, you need to consider how you will decide which student will get to take home the final product.

How-Tos

1. Before explaining the process of papier-mâché, discuss the basic "skeleton" of the creations with students. Tell them to visualize the basic shape of the animal, and to use balled up newspaper, plastic grocery bags, clothes hangers, and masking tape to create the skeleton. For example (see animals at right), the snake was made by twisting a clothes hanger into the general shape of the snake, and then wrapping wadded newspaper around it. Masking tape

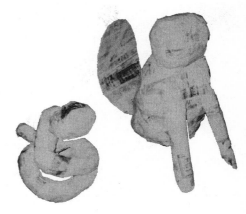

★TEACHER TIP

You might consider having the art teacher conduct this activity during the course of your state unit.

keeps the wadded paper in place. The beaver was made by stuffing a plastic grocery bag with newspaper (for the body), and adding a ball of newspaper for the head, which was then taped to the body. The cardboard tubes from paper towel rolls are used for the legs and a cardboard oval for the tail.

You might want to help your students determine which materials will best work for the basic skeletons of their animals.

2. After students have finished creating the skeleton of their animals, it is time to begin the papier-mâché process. First, students should cover their work space with newspaper for easy cleanup.

3. Next they should tear a bunch of newspaper into one-inch strips.

4. Make the papier-mâché paste by mixing $\frac{1}{2}$ cup of flour, a teaspoon of salt, and 1 cup of water. The consistency should be thick and creamy with no lumps.

5. They can use their hands to spread some of the paste onto a section of their animal, and then lay strips of newspaper over it. They should then spread some more paste over the strips. Have students continue doing this until the entire animal is covered with four layers of paper and paste.

6. Add a final layer of blank newsprint over the entire animal to prevent the newspaper from showing through their paint. Allow time for this to dry.

7. Students can then use tempera or craft paint to paint their animals. If possible, provide a selection of craft materials, such as feathers, pom-poms, pipe cleaners, buttons, straight pins with colored heads, sequins, glitter, and dimensional paints for your students to add to the animals after the paint has dried.

8. Have students do a mini-research project on the animal they created by having them complete the graphic organizer on page 59. Students can then give an oral report based on the information they collected.

Papier-Mâché Zoos
Graphic Organizer

In bold letters, write the name of the animal you picked in the circle. Use articles, books, and encyclopedias to find information about this animal to complete the graphic organizer.

In what kind of environment does it live?

How does it defend/protect itself?

How long does it live?

What does it eat?

Who are its predators?

How big does it get?

Is it a mammal, reptile, insect, or amphibian?

What are its social habits?
Is it solitary or found in groups?

What are its distinguishing features?

Other interesting facts:

How many babies does it have at one time?
How does it care for its young?

Window Box Reports

Window Box Reports are a wonderful way to display leaves and flowers from the plant life native to your state.

Materials

• manila file folders • construction paper • plastic wrap • spray glue • colored markers

Getting Started

Decide if you want the window box reports to focus on trees, shrubs, and/or flowers that can be found in your state.

Take your students on a nature walk around the neighborhood (or on a field trip to a state park) and point out the trees, shrubs, and flowers that grow in your state. Tell them that they will be doing a report on one of the plants.

Discuss important terms and concepts that they should be familiar with, such as types of seeds and how they are spread, deciduous and coniferous trees, and annual and perennial flowers.

How-Tos

1. Give each student a file folder, a sheet of 9" x 12" construction paper, and a sheet of plastic wrap.

2. First, have students cut off the small tag that sticks out from the file folder to make the edge even.

3. Next, students should measure in 1½" from all four edges of the construction paper and draw a pencil line. They should then cut this box out.

4. Cover the construction paper frame with spray glue and have students work in pairs to lay the sheet of plastic down so it sticks well. They should cut the excess plastic wrap from the edges of the construction paper.

5. Once this is done, students should collect leaves, seeds, and/or flowers from the plant on

⭐TEACHER TIP

If each student reports on a different plant, the diversity of the plant life makes for a beautifully varied bulletin board display.

which they will be reporting. They should not use sticks or anything that is too thick, such as protruding flowers or extremely large leaves. (Look at the sample shown below.)

Spray the cover of the file folder with spray glue and have students press the leaves, seeds, and flowers onto the cover so they create an attractive arrangement.

6. If the foliage does not cover too much area, you can press the window box frame over the leaves so that it sticks to the folder's cover. Otherwise, you may have to apply another coat of spray glue to the leaves and then stick them on the window box. The leaves will show through the plastic wrap and create an attractive cover for their Window Box Report.

7. Students should open the file folder. On the left-hand side they should draw and color a picture of the plant on which they are reporting. (You might have them do this before they create the window box display on the cover, especially if the plant is bulky. It is usually not a problem when working with plants that have thin leaves or flowers.)

8. On the right-hand side, they should write facts about the plant they chose. Some things they might consider discussing are the plant's scientific name; its origins; it's size and shape; the climate in which it grows best; how it propagates; whether it is an annual, biennial, or perennial; what its flowers look like and when it blooms; the types of leaves and seeds it has; and its uses.

9. Hang the Window Boxes on the bulletin board to bring the outdoors into the classroom.

CRAPE MYRTLE

CRAPE MYRTLE FACTS

- **Deciduous** — Crape Myrtles are deciduous, which means they lose their leaves in winter.
- **Climate** — Crape Myrtles like warm climates and grow best down in the South.
- **Origins** — These trees are native to Taiwan and China, but they're very popular in the U.S.
- **Latin Name** — The scientific name for crape myrtle is Lagerstroemia indica.
- **Size** — Crape myrtles are slow-growing and grow to be between 10-30 feet.
- **Shape** — They can be pruned to be bushes or can become multi-trunked or single-stemmed trees.
- **Flowers** — Large clusters of flowers cover the tree throughout late summer. Each bloom has hundreds of smaller flowers which are ruffled like crepe-paper. They can be pink, red, lavender, or white.

State Outline Maps
Patterns

Alaska

Montana

Oregon

Washington

Idaho

Nevada

Utah

California

Arizona

New Mexico

Hawaii

State Outline Maps
Patterns

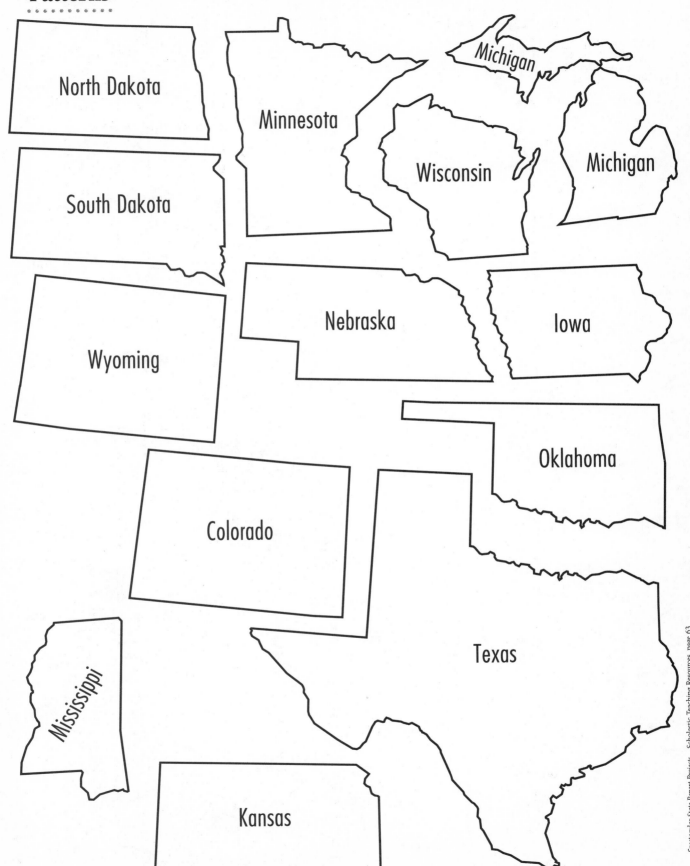

North Dakota

Minnesota

Michigan

South Dakota

Wisconsin

Michigan

Wyoming

Nebraska

Iowa

Oklahoma

Colorado

Texas

Mississippi

Kansas

Spectacular State Report Projects, Scholastic Teaching Resources, page 63

State Outline Maps
Patterns
. . . .

Illinois

Indiana

Vermont

New Hampshire

Maine

New York

Rhode Island

Maine

Massachusetts

Missouri

Pennsylvania

Connecticut

Delaware

New Jersey

Louisiana

Maryland

Ohio

West Virginia

Virginia

Kentucky

North Carolina

Tennessee

Arkansas

Florida

South Carolina

Alabama

Georgia